A Whisper in My Ear

Believe and you will give

love and peace to many.

Love 2 Light
Maggie Stark

piercearrowms@gmail.com

A Whisper in My Ear

Spirit Writings Given to

Maggie Stark

2010
Galde Press
Lakeville, Minnesota, U.S.A.

First Edition
First Printing, 2010

Galde Press
PO Box 460
Lakeville, Minnesota 55044–0460
www.galdepress.com

A Whisper In My Ear
Spirit Writings
Given to Maggie Stark

Introduction

It is with great humility and gratitude that I share my writings from Spirit. In a period of just over one year I was compelled to spontaneously produce these writings that materialized as my fingers touched the keyboard. I had no forethought or concept of what was being typed. I was stunned to see what had been written as I read the final product. Some would label this channeled, inspirational, or automatic writing.

The original copy of my writings on November 24 and 29 of 2005 have an anomaly in the color of the print which I have not been able to duplicate or explain! The dates on some of the writings have a significance as they correlate with miraculous events. I will leave that discovery to the reader.

Another interesting anecdote is that I normally make many reversals of letters when typing and I had none with these inspired or automatic writings. As I was organizing the writings into a book format there were coincidentally seven distinct topics. The number seven is a highly spiritual number, evidenced by seven chakras, seven days of creation, seven virtues, seven deadly sins, seven planes of existence etc. These writings speak to the divine within all of us, our interconnectedness, and of our destiny on this planet.

Throughout my journey I have experienced the wonders of communication with Spirit. I have been given wondrous visions of ascended masters, guides, angels, and saints throughout my life. These glorious visions remain etched in my soul. My spiritual journey brought me to the religion of Spiritualism. I am a believer in the Light and am a spiritual medium and a healer in the Spiritualist religion. I reside in Lily Dale, New York, "the World's Largest Community for the Religion of Spiritualism."

My husband Mark, who is also a medium, has been channeling my parents for five years. My beloved parents (Mary and Bill) prophesied that I would be writing and publishing this book and that at a later date more writings would follow. I look forward to that day.

I feel that a new age of awakening is dawning and that we all have a part to play. These writings are my small contribution to the new dawn that is coming.

— Namaste

OCTOBER 16, 2005

Dear Children,

Why have thou art forsaken me? It Is I who am the truth, the way and the light. Come unto me and I will giveth to you all that you need. Do not fear or want for anything. The creator loves you and will protect you. It is in the stars that all is well. Let us not go into a dark place when there is light abounding.

Do not forget that you are one with me and I with you. The heavens and the earth were created just for you. Let go of fear and earthly desires. You will become one with the father and myself in the end times. Forgiveth your neighbor and open your heart to one another. We are cut from the same cloth. It

is worn by all of us and protects and shelters us. Have no
doubt when the wonders are all around you. Look towards
the sun, the moon and the stars to give proof of my love for
you. This is a time of great change and enlightenment for all
who believe. The veil is getting thinner and more transparent
than at any other time. You are my child and I am your loving and protecting father.

Go beyond the stars, the Milky Way, the galaxies and the
many universes and you will see my face. It is a face that
emits love, forgiveness, peace, and harmony. Try to envision
my face upon yours and act accordingly. It is possible to
indeed have heaven upon earth if you so desire. The birds,
the skies, the rainbows, are all smiling upon you. Take the
time to see the sacredness in every living creature. See the
white light that is emitted from every living creature, the
rocks, the soil, the waters, the flowers all manner of living
beings. It is truly a wondrous sight to behold. See the light
that shines from a newborn animal or baby's eyes. It is the
light from mine eyes. Oh can't you witness that all things are
sacred. It is from the divine with whence we came. The
breath you take is infused with the love and light of the
almighty. It is he who wants you to flourish in all aspects of
your life and being. It is He who wants nothing but the high-
est and best for all of His children. You are from love and will
return to love. Let the outstretched hands of the Creator hold
you, nourish, you and protect you. It is the home from

whence you came and will return again.

Namaste.... recognize the sacredness and light in all of you.

Remembering Who We Are

October 19, 2005

My Dear Ones,

It is a time of sorrow and a time of joy. Do not be saddened
by what is all about you. Rejoice in what is to come. Your soul
and spirit will triumph in the end. Let love be the level from
which you build your foundation. Fear not what may come.
It is only one step in a journey of many steps. Your savior has
a magnificent plan for each of you. We cannot fathom the
depths as to his love for us. One day you will perceive an
infinitesimal piece of the expanding and unending puzzle of
which you are just a piece. It is not yours for the understanding or knowing. It is for you to only exist in this earthly plane
and for all eternity.

The Father has so much in the heavens to share with you his beloved ones. Do not question but accept all he has and will give to you. If you could know the heart of the creator there would be no war, turmoil, fear, or doubt. All I ask is that you believe. Love is the answer to all questions. Do not recoil in doubt but rejoice in the knowing of the love the creator has for you. Extend your hands out to the creator so that he may infuse you with his love and make you one with him. Let the dove, the holy spirit send his light out to you. May the holy spirit be above you always…always, watching, guiding, and loving you. Look upwards to the heavens for this is from whence you came. You are more wondrous than the brightest star, the most radiant planet or the warmest sun. Look also within your heart to see the face of the creator warming your heart and very being with his divine and everlasting love. By loving me you love yourself. We are one. Never forget the interconnectedness with which we shall always share.

Love always

OCTOBER 23, 2005

Dear Children,

It is with great joy and love that I come to you. You are the reason for the existence of all life. You transcend all that the universe is made of. You are the stars, the heavens, and the seas. You are the image of me. You are the light and the love from which all else emanates.

Shine your love and light upon whatever may come your way. Do not hide in a dark place but lighten the path of every living creature that you encounter. You will some day know the light and the way to me. You will travel back to your true home where I will be waiting to greet you with open arms.

You will be received by all who have loved you and whom you have loved. Do not fear, you are never alone. Spirit is always with you. We guide you, protect and love you so you may take the path of light which will return you to your true home. You may not live in a grand palace in this existence but a mansion of love awaits all who believe and trust in me.

Open your heart, think less with your mind; this will put you upon your true path. Material gains, pleasures, and fame are not what you are here for. You are here to serve and love one another. You are here to grow and learn so your soul may reach new heights. You are here to lift one another up; to ascend to a higher level of being. Take the time to be aware of all I have given you. Let your five senses be awash with the love and beauty which has been put before you on this earth. Revere all. Let your sixth sense open your heart and your chakras so that I may enter your ethereal body.

Feel the love which is given to you unconditionally. Feel the knowing that you are me and I am you. Feel the connectedness with which we share. Feel the beautiful gift I have given to you, which is eternal life. Hold your head high so that I may gaze upon your beauteous face which mirrors thine. When you see a winged creature hover around you know that I am there. When you hear a beautiful waterfall, know that I am there. When you taste the freshness of a fruit, know that I am there. When your neighbor smiles at you, assists you know that I am there. When you feel the warmth of a hug, know that I am there. I am in all things so that you do not forget from whence you came.

Let the light enter and emanate from you so that all may see the path which is there for all to follow. It will lead you to the eternal light, which is your true home.

Namaste

I humbly thank Spirit for channeling this message to me through automatic writing on Oct. 23, 2005.

Please remember these healing words whenever you are feeling alone, lost, or frightened. Know that the Creator is there for you.

OCTOBER 29, 2005

$\mathcal{D}ear$ $\mathcal{O}nes,$

Let us give thanks to the Creator. He and only he alone understands the mysteries of the universe. Do not trouble yourself with asking the WHY, the WHAT, the WHEN, and the HOW of existence. Trust that it is all given to you with love.

There is no need to ponder the limitless questions that are presented before you. Trust that you will be taken care of. The creator wraps you in his arms and cradles your everlasting soul. Trouble yourself no longer with questioning your existence. Just know that it is. Live in the moment. Live in love.

Live a limitless life of abundance, truth, and beauty. Give of
yourself to one another. Take the time to know the beauty in
one another. Realize that you are not alone in this voyage. I
am the captain of the ship and will protect my charges. Even
though the seas of life may be rough at times do not fear, I
am forever at the helm.

The stars and the light of truth are guiding all of us. So go
into that night sky knowing that you are more loved than the
countless constellations and universes that will ever exist. The
heavenly Father has one purpose and that is to give you everlasting life. Believe and all is given to you.

Each of you is as precious as every grain of sand is. There is
no separation of the divine. It is in all things.

Namaste

Bartholomew

October 30, 2005

$\mathcal{D}ear\ \mathcal{O}nes,$

It is now time for all man to go within and connect to the
Creator. Do not think that you are alone. You are not. You are
one with me. I am you, you are me. It is with that belief that
you may go forward and live a life of peace, harmony, and
gentleness.

It is enough to know that the Creator gave you everlasting
life. It is enough to know that you are precious. It is enough
to know that you are given the gift of eternal life. It is enough
to know that you are loved. It is enough to know that you will
be with the Creator always.

It is your free will which will determine the ascent of your soul to be closer to the Creator. It is free will which is the lesson that we must all learn. It is free will which by every action we can show our love for the Creator. It is by free will that we can make the Earth a better place.

Our every action interacts and affects every being on the planet. Our every action will some day be the mirror and image of our soul which we will have to view. Let us know that all we do, say, and think is reflected back to us and out into the universe. There is no I, but a collective We. As I look down upon thee I have hope for the future that man will recognize the beauty and love which I have provided for him.

Every man has the power to change the world and the course of future events. There is no hopelessness, there is only light if you choose to follow it. It is your decision to live in darkness or to live in light. See me with my arms outstretched, my face smiling and my heart full of love to you. Come to me your Father.

Ezekiel

NOVEMBER 2, 2005

Beloved,

It is I who am the way to the light and the truth. Do not be
fooled by the naysayer who would wish to discount my love
for you. I have not abandoned you in your hour of need. I
will always be there for my beloved children.

Never doubt my everlasting love for you. You are the one for
whom the universe is made. You are the one for whom the
rivers flow, the stars shine, and the soil gives life. You are the
epitomé of my handiwork and creation. See myself in your
reflection. Know that I am inside of you, outside of you, and
all around you. Know that the Creator wants to share his

being with you. He wants to shower you with all he has created.

Do not waste your time on this earth plane by forgetting why you were created, and the everlasting love and life he has promised and will give to you. Know in your heart that there could be indeed paradise on earth if you so desire. Just look at the wonders that surround you. Know that goodness is emanating from all creation. Know that you matter, you are the reason for the dawn of creation.

God so loved you he made you in his likeness. Spread his divine message to all you meet. Let the love of the creator break into a trillion rays of light and bathe the universe with the white light of love. Remember I am one with you, the universe, and the eternal light.

Namaste

Raphael

Straying From the Path

NOVEMBER 9, 2005

Dear Ones,

It is not your time to wonder and fret about the condition of the world. Only know that I am there for you always. There may be strife, poverty, war and natural disasters, but they are only a minute piece of existence. You shall have everlasting life so do not worry for your safety. Wars, famine, man's inhumanity to man is only a stage upon which the drama of life is played out.

In order for growth there must be conflict. Man has to be able to use his free will to become closer to the Creator. I know you do not understand the meaning of my words now but I assure you, you will. Do not think you have been forsaken when you see the darkness that exists. There must be darkness for light to exist. There must be pain for joy to exist. Lift your head and eyes upward to see the never-ending and infinite abundance which awaits you. Do not become frightened thinking I have forsaken you. You will always find peace within yourself for I am there always with you. Go with the knowledge that your individual actions may clear the darkness and let the light of love shine brightly. You make a difference.

Your every action, thought and feeling all affect the balance of existence. You have the choice each day to go towards the light and love or to deepen the darkness that is presently on the earth. My eyes cry tears of sorrow for what you have made of the earth plane. You have traveled so far off the path that was set out for you. You may start anew on that path by putting one foot in front of the other with the intent of peace, love, and harmony. There is always reformation to each and every soul. The door is never shut on my children. The key to opening the door is to love one another as I love you. When the door is opened for you, you will finally understand and realize how great my love is for you.

You will see the light that will bathe your soul in my love.

Please go forward on the path so that you may reach that

golden door which promises you more than you can ever imagine on the earth plane. When you see my face and my hands extended out to you, you will know that of which I speak .

Love to the earth, my children and all that exists.

November 24, 2005

Dear Ones,

How have I failed you? In what way do you not know me? Do you not see me in everything about you? Is it not enough that I give you life, the beautiful earth plane, the stars, the moons and the heavens?

What more proof do I need to show you for you to believe in my love for you? Is it not enough that my son died for you? Is it not enough that I cry tears of sorrow for the way you are abusing the Earth and one another? Is it not enough that I cry out for you to hear me. Is it not enough that I am sending messengers to Earth to help you see the light and the way?

Is it not enough that I am lifting the veil for you to see that I am real. Is it not enough that I am offering you everlasting love, and salvation for your eternal soul? Is it not enough that I am present in all that is around you from the smallest atom to the solar systems?

Is it not enough that I gift you with a beautiful ever-present sunrise and sunset? Is it not enough that I have placed the moon, the stars, and the planets in the night sky so that you might feel my presence? Is it not enough that at the moment of the miracle of birth I am with you? Is it not enough that at the end of your earthly existence I am there with you?

Faith. That is the gift you must give to yourself and to one another in order for you to see me clearly.

Hope is the light that will bring you to me even in times of darkness.

Charity will be the actions and the way of life which will bring you to heaven's door and back to me your heavenly father. A father will never abandon his children, and I will never abandon you, my dear ones. Believe and all is possible.

Namaste

November 29, 2005

Beloved,

What art thou waiting for? Art thou waiting for definitive proof that I exist? Are you waiting to see the sun dance in the sky? Are you waiting for the seas to part, the heavens to fall from the sky? What is it you need for you to have faith and belief in me? Do I need to send angels from on high to line the streets for you to believe? Do I need to send you the departed ones on the other side to show you that life is eternal? Do I need to send you spirit on the wings of a dove for you to realize that life is everlasting? Your soul is eternal. I am with you always. Never doubt my love for you.

Know that you will know in your heart that I am always present with you. Feel the love that warms your spirit. Feel the grace that is always there for you. You only have to ask. You only have to ask for grace, for salvation, and the path to me will be lit. Do not be fooled by the kings of this earthly plane that wish to trivialize the spiritual and elevate the physical gains of this earthly plane to new exalted heights. Know that there is only one path to follow. That path is lit by the virtues of kindness, truth, faith, hope, and charity. Come out of the shadows and bask in my glorious light. Let me see your beautiful soul. Let the light shine brightly on you, my beloved children. There is only one home and only one path to it.

Most of all, shine your light to all who are on the path toward their one true home. The sun rises each morning to remind you of the light in your soul and the light on your true path home.

Namaste

DECEMBER 4, 2005

My Dear Ones,

Is it not time to be thankful? Is it not time to be aware that I
am there for you? Is it not time to know that I am with you
always? Is it not time to know that I am longing for your
love? Is it not time to know that I am disappointed in the way
that you have squandered the gifts of the Earth that have
been given to you? Is it not time to know that I am shocked
at how you have disregard for one another, and for the creatures that have been bestowed upon you?

Is it not time to know that I am lamenting about how you
have chosen earthly desires over spiritual desires? Is it not

time to know that I am begging you to look within and see
my presence in each of you? Is it not time to know that I am
imploring you to be kind to all of the Creator's creatures and
to all living things on the Earth? Is it not time to look
towards the heavens and realize that your behavior is affect-
ing all the universe?

You are connected to all of the stars, just as the stars of the
constellation of Orion are connected, don't you see that you
are not alone? There are limitless vistas for you to explore.
There is no time, no space. There is no end. I know that that
is difficult for you to comprehend. Just know that it is so. Just
know that you are and always will be. I have offered before
you everlasting life; not just in this earthly plane but in many
other countless dimensions. The next time you greet a friend,
a neighbor or family member, know that I am present.

Acknowledge the divine in all. Acknowledging the divine in
all will assist you in reaching your divine potential. This will
have a ripple effect on all of the universe. You are but one
pinpoint of light, but cumulatively you are the beacon which
shines on the path to your true eternal home. Do not forget
from whence you came and will come again for all eternity. I
will be waiting to greet you with love in my heart and my
arms wide open. You will be with our true father once again.

Namaste
Bartholomew

December 11, 2005

Dear Ones,

It is time to rejoice. It is time to remember the gifts that have been given to you. It is time to acknowledge the presence of the divine in each of you. It is time to know that you have a duty and responsibility to the Earth and to one another. It is time to know that you are the keeper of the future.

You are the keeper of the truth, the light, and the way. You and only you can make a difference. You and only you can set upon the path toward goodness and light. You and only you can lift your heart and your will toward the light that is enveloping you in everlasting love and peace. You and only you can change the course of history. You and only you can make this a heaven upon Earth, which was intended by the creator.

You are so far off the path it will take much effort and determination for man to regain his footing on the path of light which has always been set before him. It is your free will which has led you to stray so far from your heavenly father. He will never shut the door on his children but he is saddened by the choices that you have made. You are not honoring the divine within you, which is denying his existence. It is difficult for the creator to observe all the harm, misdeeds and mistreatment that you have done to one another and to all his creatures and creations.

You are always striving to boost yourself and your ego to insurmountable earthly and temporary physical goals. You do not see the road that is ahead of you. You are blocked by your self-serving ego, hedonism and earthly desires. You do not acknowledge the spiritual reality, only the physical reality. How surprised you will be to finally see what I have planned for your everlasting life. You will reflect upon your earthly existence and see how you foolishly spent the gift of precious life that was given to you. Existence on the earth plane is meant to be a lesson which will expand the growth of your soul. It is meant to give you the vehicle and means to come closer to your heavenly Creator.

Do not disappoint him further by making unwise choices

while you are on the Earth. Rise to the expectations that the creator has for you and know that you can surpass those expectations if you only see the divine and me within one another. All things are possible and limitless when you believe.

Namaste

Bartholomew

December 17, 2005

My Children,

Go unto the world and teach the ways of the holy spirit. Let man know that I am the way, the truth, and their salvation.

Go unto the world and know that I am preparing a home for each of you. A home that you cannot begin to imagine. A home that will be forever. A home that will have love, kindness, and serenity. A home like none other.

I beseech you to listen to the Creator: do his bidding to do his work, to light the way for all to follow, to be the instrument for spirit to be channeled. It is you and you alone who can manifest the love and the goodness that God has bestowed upon you.

You must unwrap it as if it is a precious gift. You must treasure it and realize it's worth. You must share this gift with all of God's creatures and creations. You must be the keeper of this gift. You must make sure that this gift is known to future generations and is cherished.

It is a great responsibility that the light workers of the Earth must undertake. It is only when the way and the truth are known that man, and the creatures of the Earth, might be saved.

It is only when man realizes that he is the gift. He is the gift to himself and to all of God's creatures. He is the gift that is the most cherished of all God's bounty. He is the reflection of the Creator and of all that is good and holy. Remember to cherish yourself for you are the gift from God and to God. All is one with the holy spirit.

Remember, my children, love is the way to your home. Love is the essence of your existence and essential to your salvation. Love one another as I love you my children.

Namaste

DECEMBER 25, 2005

Beloved,

Let us not forget why we are celebrating this sacred day. It is a day to symbolize and remember from whence we came. To remember who created us, who loves us, and who will always shelter us. It is a day to remember that no one is ever alone. We have both the family of man and the family of God. We are so blessed to be wanted and to be loved by our fellow man and the Creator.

It is a time to look at the face of your neighbor, brother, and to see my face superimposed upon their faces. It is a time to relinquish any thoughts of selfishness, pride, greed, or hatred.

It is a time to sow the seeds of love, peace and harmony. It is a time to accept all the graces that the Creator can and will bestow upon you just for the asking. It is a time to see your purpose on this plane, to see that your acts and deeds or misdeeds will determine your position and place with the Creator.

It is a time for knowing, for realization for an awakening of your true potential which will serve both yourself, your brother, and the Creator. It is a time to let the holy spirit and the love of the creator into your heart. It is a time to release the love the holy spirit has infused you with. It is a time to share that love with all of the Creator's creatures. It is a time to remember that the universe is limitless in all the benign gifts that could both be bestowed upon you and your neighbor just for the asking. Intention is the key to salvation and abounding happiness. It is when you serve one another and the Creator that true happiness can be found. Your intention is the key to the unlimited bounty that can and will be bestowed upon you and your brother. Do unto others as you would have them do unto you is the key that will open the gates of heaven to you. Live by those words and you will have assurance of entrance into the kingdom of heaven. Namaste to all you encounter.

Live by example, and with love in your heart. Enjoy this special day that was so created just for you and the days to come.

Returning to the Path

DECEMBER 30, 2005

Dear Ones,

Is it any wonder that you feel alone, abandoned and unloved, when you refuse to acknowledge my existence? Is it any wonder that you want for material goods to fill the deep cavern that is in your soul? Is it any wonder that you feel disconnected, purposeless, and depressed when you go about your daily existence? Is it any wonder that you do not see your reason for living, you do not see all that I have created for you? Is it any wonder that you try to fill the endless void in your heart with meaningless pursuit of material goods, accomplishments that build your ego and a never-ending feeling of little satisfaction with your day-to-day life? To recognize my existence and the plan that I have for you will fill your heart and soul with light and love?

As banal and basic as that sounds, it is so. Take your blinders off, for the first time really see what is presented before you in the beauty of Nature, creatures, the cycles of life, the seasons, the heavens and the stars. Really see what the Creator has laid out upon your path to him. See that the roads are paved with endless opportunities to help your fellow man and to contribute to the planet in a positive way. See that you are connected to one another and that you are not alone. See that there are signs along your path to guide you to the heavenly father. See that you are not alone, but that your heavenly father has laid out many paths to reach him. You may presently be on the wrong path.

There is always opportunity to right your path. Ask for guidance in the form of prayer and contemplation. Listen to the voice in your heart that quietly whispers the truth. Listen and look for the signs that are all about you. Your guides and loved ones on the other side are upon each shoulder, ready to show you the way. Remember that we all stumble upon the path of life but there is always someone there to pick us up and dust us off. Remember that that someone is me, your heavenly father. It is my intent that all my children will find their path back to me. I must have all my children with me to be complete.

We are one in the same and will always be. Love one another and yourself, and you will be loving me.

Namaste

JANUARY 8, 2006

$\mathcal{D}ear$ $\mathcal{O}nes,$

Let us not forget to enjoy the beauty that is ours and all around us. Let us not forget that our five senses were given to us for a reason. That reason being to enjoy all the physical beauty in vision, sound, taste, touch, and smell that the Creator has given to us. He wants you to enjoy the world and universe he has created for you. He wants you to appreciate, minute by minute, the gift of life he has bestowed upon you.

Look upwards and see his spirit in the rays of the sun, rays coming from the clouds, birds hovering, the sun rising, and the sun setting. See with your own eyes what he has given to you. Do not have blinders on as you live your life. See what was meant to be seen. Enjoy the daily activities of life, preparing your food, eating, taking care of the bodily instrument he has given to you. Treasure your body, nourish the physical as well as the spiritual aspects of your existence.

Keep your eye upon your heavenly father, guides and angels who are there to comfort, direct, and be there with you always. See not only with your physical eye but with your third eye. Reach out and touch those that you love, which would and should be your fellow man. Touch their hearts with your love, touch their lives with your concern. May your intent be to touch everyone you meet in a positive way.

Mother Teresa was an example of this virtue. She touched everyone, even those who were deemed untouchable. Become an ambassador of love from the heavenly father. Become an example to your fellow man. Become the being that you were meant to be and can be. Life is given to only a select few. You are selected by the heavenly father to have this precious gift. Realize its implications and importance. You are given the gift of eternal life. Trust that it is eternal and that you are one with the Father. Enjoy the day, each and every one. Make the world a better place for all creatures.

Abundance is possible. There are no limitations to your existence in this life and in the next. Trust that you are loved and cared for and your life has a purpose. That purpose is to elevate your soul to the heights of the heavenly father.

Namaste

JANUARY 22, 2006

$\mathcal{D}ear \; \mathcal{O}nes,$

It is now the time to examine what is meaningful to you in
your life. You only have the hours in a day to accomplish your
life's work. What is that life's work? Is it to raise a family, to
help the needy, to spread my word? You have many choices to
make in this lifetime.

Choose wisely. Earth is the school where your soul lessons are
learned. It is the place where your soul grows and comes closer to the Creator. It can also be the place where you are sepa-
rated from the Creator and all the good that he has planned
for you on this time on Earth. Remember to view each day as

a lesson. Each day there are circumstances, people, and events from which you are meant to learn. Let your relationships teach you the way to me. Let your every action reflect my love for you and humanity.

The old saying that you are your brother's keeper is so simple yet so true.

There is time on your side. Use your time wisely. It is such a privilege to be on earth and to be able to grow and learn. You take the sun rising and the sun setting with such little thought to the miraculous being that is creating it just for you. Just remember that I am behind all of the sunsets, sunrises, stars, galaxies, and moons. Take the time to go within and see me in your heart. See my face in your mind. See my love for you reflected in your own eyes. See my love for you reflected in the eyes of your fellow man.

You need to take the time, the moment to be still and to look for me. I have not forsaken you. I am within you, about you, and am trying to show you the way to me. Listen with your heart and your very soul. I will be whispering to you the words and the way which will lead you to me, your Father.

Namaste

FEBRUARY 5, 2006

Beloved,

Let the little children know the truth. Let the children know that there is light and love in this world. Let them know that there is the possibility of peace on this Earth. Let them know that mine will be done. Let them see by your example what love is like. Let them see what truth is. Let them see what can be. Let them hear my divine voice within theirs. Let them feel my love for them.

It is you and only you who can instruct the children in the way of love, hope, and charity. Presently they are not seeing the best that man has to offer. They are seeing the dark side of humanity in all the media, politics, and entertainment that is all about them. Let the light seep into their present dark world. Let them see that there is goodness and love all about them and within them. Let them know that I am one with them. Block out all the negative images that are clouding their minds and soul. Let them know there is hope for the future. They have control of what happens to themselves in this lifetime. They have power to spread the word and the light of God. They have the opportunity to be the light workers of tomorrow.

It is by your example of basking in and emanating the light of God that the way will be lit for the younger generation. Do not be afraid to stand up for what is right, what is true. The children need a teacher of light and love. They do not need to be under the masters of darkness. Rise up and let your love shine through the darkness.

Namaste

FEBRUARY 21, 2006

My Dear Ones,

It is time for you to look up and realize that I have been watching you from afar and near. Do you not see that I am right beside you as well as in the heavens and stars? I am always close to you. Be still and listen for my voice. Open your eyes and see that I am there. Reach out and touch my guiding hand. Feel my love for you always.

Know that it is not your imagination. It is real, I am real, you are real. We exist within and with one another. We are forever entwined in this dance called life. Life is never-ending, and ever entwining. We are joined together for all eternity. You are part of the Holy Trinity. The breath of your soul exists in the Father, Son and Holy spirit. Remember that your evolution depends on how you enhance your soul on the earth plane. Make good use of your numbered days on the Earth.

Each day is a gift to contribute to the whole soul growth of humanity. Just remember me when you see the sun rise and the sun set. I am in the rays that awaken and lull you to sleep.

Go in peace and love, my dear ones. Your Father is there for you always.

The Reflection of the Light

March 12, 2006

Dear Ones,

Let your heart be open and full. Let your arms reach out to all who are near. Let your words be those of love and healing. Let your thoughts have positive intentions. Let your hands do my work. Let your ears hear the voice of mine. Let your fears and doubts go. Let your frustrations and worries wither by the wayside. Let your spirit know that this life on the earth plane is a lesson in which your soul will have the opportunity to grow. Let your brothers and sisters know that we are all of one family.

Your heavenly father sits at the head of our communal table.

He only wants the best for all of his children. Know in your heart that there is goodness in each and every one of his children. Know that free will is the test by which our heavenly progression is measured. Know that each day is a test. Each day is a test of your free will and the choices you make.

Make sure that you choose wisely. Make sure that in your life review you will be joyous when your actions, thoughts, and intentions are mirrored back to you. Make sure that you are the reflection of your heavenly Creator when you meet his presence face to face. Please remember that you were created in his image. Make your final image reflect his love, peace, and harmony and forgiveness which he has given freely to you. Remember that we are one with the heavenly Father.

Go in peace and love my beloved children.

Namaste

MARCH 19, 2006

Dear Ones,

Do not fear. Do not fear that I have abandoned you. I am here. I am here in the before, the present and the after. You also have this gift of everlasting life and a union with me. Do not fear when you look within and you have not found me yet. I am there.

You must push aside your emotions which keep you from finding true peace, love, and joy. When you find these things, you will find me within your heart. Emotions are a barrier to true love, peace, and happiness. Emotions make you react to your world rather than to just *be*.

To be in this world you must live in the moment. Appreciate all the beauty that is surrounding you. Know that true peace comes from within. Do not react with emotion to all that happens in your life.

Accept, learn, and realize the lessons that occur in your life. These lessons will elevate your soul's progression. Always ask: What did this experience teach me? What am I to learn from the encounters, experiences, and relationships that fall or are placed before me? Nothing is random on the earth plane.

There may be the appearance of chaos, but in that chaos there is order. Remember that there are no coincidences, just the even, humming sound of the universe at work.

One day when you are one on the other side you may have an overview of the complexities of the universe, but never a full understanding of its mechanisms. Just remember that the Creator, which is the source of what is, will always be.

Namaste

April 2, 2006

Dear Ones,

It is your responsibility to give light and love to this world. You are the ones who must make a difference. You are the ones who have been trusted with this great and loving responsibility. It is time for you to act. It is time for you to teach. It is time for you to heal. It is a time of great change in this world. It is time for you to make known my love and caring for all of my children. It is time for you to look within, and see the divinity in all of you. It is time to look within and share your love and light with all whom you meet.

See my face reflected in the face of your neighbor.

Mirror back my love for you which is present in all who live.
Make your reflection one of love, peace, and harmony. Make
your reflection one with mine. Just like the prisms in a crys-
tal, one by one your reflection will refract and shower the
planet with a glow of love and peace. You are but a prism in
which my love will reflect and be refracted out into the universe.

There is the essence of my love in each in every one of you.
By sharing yourself with the world you will be making my
love for all creation known. Again, it is time, share your light
and love with the world. You are my light workers.

Namaste

APRIL 16, 2006

Beloved,

Touch your forehead, touch your heart, touch your shoulders, and in doing so you are making the sign of the cross. The cross that symbolizes my love for you and the promise of eternal light and life. Do not look upon the cross as my sole accomplishment or legacy to you. Look upon the deeds of my life to illuminate your path. Look upon the miracles that I performed, the loaves and fishes that were multiplied, the prophecies, the healings.

Just remember that all you must do is ask and you shall receive. Abundance can and will be yours if you only ask.

Remember that as I can do, so can you. My gifts, my divinity are in all of you.

You just need to go within to find my presence. The kingdom of God is there in all of its glory within you. The key to the kingdom is love, love for yourself, for me and for your fellow man and all God's creatures.

Know that you too can glimpse the divine plan that has been provided for you. Know too that you have the ability to manifest abundance in your life and in the lives of others. Know too that you have the gift of healing. Let the gift of healing flow from your hands and heart. Know too that the Creator has given man the ability to prophesize and heal. Know too that many have been glimpses into the heavenly realm. Know too that the mystical and beautiful visions you have been given of me, my angels, my blessed mother and saints are real. They do exist.

The veil is becoming more and more transparent and is opening so that you may know of my and your future heavenly existence. There is indeed a heavenly kingdom that awaits you. Build your equity on the earth plane so that you may have the palace you deserve in my heavenly kingdom. The law of cause and effect is what governs your ascent into the heavenly kingdom.

Natural law is real. Natural law is what balances your existence and is the gyroscope of the universe. Natural law and adherence to it will help you find your way back to your heavenly father and home. Go in peace and love.

When you see the sunrise and sunset know that I am there with my divine and guiding light to protect my beloved children.

Namaste

May 14, 2006

Dear Ones,

It is the time to know. It is the time to feel. It is the time to see. It is the time to hear. It is the time for you to know me. It is the time to know yourself. It is the time for change. It is the time to share your gifts with the world. It is the time to come forth and share my teachings with those you meet. It can be sharing in a small way, not in a spectacular way. It can be the helping hand you extend to your neighbor, the smile you give to a clerk, a hug you give to a child. It is time for me to work through you.

Let me share grace with you so that you may radiate it out to those you touch. Let me give hope to those who are hopeless. Let me give love to those who are loveless. Let me give strength to those who are weak. All things are possible when there is faith, knowing and belief.

The universe is abundant with all that you desire and need. You just must believe. You are not on earth to suffer. You are on earth to manifest with love and a high vibrational energy. If only you believed, if each and every soul on this plane believed, there would be heaven on Earth. There would be an abundance for everyone. There would be no famine, crime or hardships. I would be walking amongst and with each and every one of you. You would be aware of my presence, you would feel my love for you. You would see my love reflected in every soul, animal and creation. You would know that I am part of you and you with me.

There would be no separation or divisions, there would be a oneness with me and the universe. When I look at the earth it brings tears to my eyes that you do not see me within your-selves. You have gone off the path into an isolated dark place. You have given up hope, you have given up faith that the earth could vibrate with the love that I have for my children.

Children, do not despair; look deep into your heart, know that I am there. Take the time to look for my presence in every soul, creature and plant that is upon the Earth. Know that there are mysteries you cannot fully understand but the intent of existence is to bask in the glory of the Creator and all his creations. Know that it is not too late to leave the path of darkness and follow the path of light which is lovingly before you. Know that I am with you even in the darkness.

Love and Peace.

Namaste

May 28, 2006

Dear Ones,

Why are you alone? Why are you feeling that there is no hope? Why are you feeling that there is nothing but darkness about you? Why do you not see that I am around and about everything that exists? You know that if you smell a flower, pet a dog, comfort a newborn that I am there. You know that I am in all things. I am in the wind, the rain, the sun, and the clouds. I am in the rays of the sunrise and the sunset.

Lift your head to see me in the stars, the moon and the heavens. You know in your heart that you are not alone. You have your angels, guides, and spirit friends who are looking from above waiting for you to reach out to them. All you have to do is ask for their assistance and it will be given. They are there to help you along your path which will lead you to your true home, your real existence. Do not feel that you are unworthy of spiritual guidance and assistance.

Know that you are more loved than you will ever know. You are the precious gift that retains its value and joy. You are one with the father. You are one with the son and one with the Creator. You must know that you emanate from an existence that the earthly plane is just a pale copy of. There is no way for the physical plane to even give you a glimpse of what is to come on the other side. Your senses in this plane are not able to comprehend the beauty and immenseness of what the heavenly father has in store for you when you return home.

It is as if you are blind on this plane and then become sighted when you return home. Know that your father will be waiting for you with open arms. Your loved ones will be waiting with open arms to welcome you home. You will be enthralled with love and peace: peace you have never experienced in this plane. You will look back at your life on the earthly plane and realize that there is more that you could and should have done for your fellow man. You will see each deed replayed and knowing the truth will see how you fulfilled your destiny and your divine plan. My dear ones do not waste the precious time you have on this plane.

When your life review is played make sure that you are the best that you can be. Make sure that you are acting with your heart, not with your ego. Make sure that you are fulfilling your divine plan with the precious gift of life that the Creator has given to you. Make sure to make every second, minute, day, week, month and year fulfilling your divine destiny so that you too may smile when you see your life review.

Go in love and peace.

Namaste

JUNE 11, 2006

My Children,

Look up at the sun. Look up at the moon . Look up at the
stars. Look deep within your heart. The Creator is crying for
your love. He must know that you see him in every living
creature. You must go back to the old ways of mankind. You
must live in the natural world to become reconnected to the
Creator. You have become so detached from the source you
are lost.

Many years ago the buffalo was taken from us. Our lands
were taken from us. My people are lost. My people were so
connected to the source and the land; now the connection

has been broken. The ways of the Penobscot have been forgotten. It is up to each and everyone of us to work together and save this beautiful Earth which the creator has given to us. We must not squander its bounty. We must revere in its natural beauty. We must cherish the most precious gift of all: ourselves and one another. There is an order to all that exists. Man has broken this order with his greed and selfishness. Please hear and heed my plea to you. Reconnect with Mother Earth and all its beauty. Appreciate the landscape not that of a skyscraper. A cleansing is happening on the earth plane. You may not understand its immediate effect but it is happening for a reason.

The slate must be wiped clean for the new order to establish itself. You have gone so far off the path, disrupted the order so that chaos is reigning. The Creator has set in motion the cleansing that is occurring. Do not despair with the earthquakes, tornadoes, volcanoes, hurricanes, and tsunamis that are happening ever more frequently. In these disasters there is much teaching and learning that is to happen.

Do not forget that the earth plane is a school for the soul's higher attainment and development. There will be beauty and light on the other side, unlike you have ever known or even conceived of. The earth plane is a pale imitation of the true reality. My people once knew the order and plan that the Creator had for us. Our disintegration was the microcosm that is now spread throughout the Earth.

We were the first to be the example of being disconnected from Spirit. Go back to the ways of Spirit. Summon your spirit ancestors and guides to show you the way. All you must do is ask. Such a simple act as asking can change the course of your soul and of history. Do not turn your back on the spirits that are waiting to help you. Look up and see their smiling faces radiate their love for you.

Ask and it is given.

Native Elder

OCTOBER 15, 2006

Dear Ones,

Rally round one another. It is a time of cooperation and healing. Have you not known that for so long I have been watching and worrying about how you are squandering the gifts of the Earth and of the spirit? How I have watched you pursue the darker realms of existence? How I have watched you turn out and away from the light that has always been there for you?

It gives me displeasure to know that some of you have little concern for the Earth and for one another. It is now time to turn towards the light and to shut the door on darkness. You must do this if you are to save the Earth and one another. It is not your will that must be done, it is thine. Remember that every atom in life is a miracle, every ant, every proton, and every panda is a miracle from the Creator.

No one else has the power to create. You must join forces with the Creator to help his creation and co-create with him, not destroy what he has made for you. You must see beyond your immediate physical needs and think ahead for the generations that will come after you. You must leave them with an Earth that is better for your existence on it. That is true in your daily life. Every interaction you have should leave a person the better for having met and interacted with you.

Think of the way that the Christ interacted with mankind. That too should be your model for behavior. Go in love and peace.

Co-create with me.

DECEMBER 25, 2006

*D*ear *O*nes,

Today is the day that man must know what it is to be human
and humane. Today is the day that man must rise to the level
that he can ascend to. Today is the day that he must make a
new beginning to save himself and the Earth. Today is the
day that he recognizes the gifts of the Earth that he has
squandered. Today is the day that he vows to make good the
wrong that he has committed against the Earth and his fellow man. Today is the day that will mark a new beginning
for all mankind to see the glory and light that is available for
him to bask in and also emit. Today do not forget from
whence you came.

Do not forget who you are and who you have the potential to be. Do not forget that you are one with the heavenly father. Do not forget that you can make paradise upon this Earth plane by your thoughts, words, and actions. Do not waste the precious time that has been given you. Realize that life is a divine gift which is to be relished, enjoyed and revered. Relinquish negative thoughts, words and actions, let your soul soar to the heights from which it came. Today is the day when you can recognize the gift the Creator has given to you with the birth of his holy son.

His son came to Earth to be a model for humanity in which the path followed will lead man back to his heavenly home. Know that the Creator loves you and his son and has an eternal home for you. Let this day rekindle the heavenly spark that is present in all man. Do not let negativity extinguish the divine spark that affords you eternal life with the creator. Be at one with one another and the Creator.

There is only one source, one divine light and one divine eternal home. Make anew the heavenly path of thought, word and action that will ensure your place in the Creator's heavenly arms.

Go in peace and love.

The Author

Maggie Stark is a spiritual medium and healer who resides with Mark, her beloved husband of thirty-five years, in Lily Dale, New York, which is "the world's largest community for the religion of Spiritualism." Through unbelievable synchronistic events they are now residents in this beautiful and peaceful community. It is true that you never know where life and Spirit will take you.

Maggie is a native of Maine, and her spirit writings were given to her while she was residing in South Portland. For thirty-four years Maggie dedicated her life to teaching multihandicapped and autistic students.

Maggie's spiritual journey has opened her eyes, ears, and heart to the wonders of Spirit, the universe, natural law, and synchronicity. She is anxious to share her messages from Spirit so that everyone will find peace within and about them and realize the love the Creator has for all of us.

Namaste

Maggie Stark